FACES & SPACES

40 Years Aedes Architecture Forum

PARK BOOKS

1980–1988
Aedes Grolmanstraße

1988–2009
Aedes Savignyplatz

1995–2006
Aedes Hackesche Höfe

2006–2020+
Aedes Pfefferberg

This book would not have been possible without these great photographers. Thank you for lending us your eyes to get an insight into the story of Aedes:

Erik-Jan Ouwerkerk, Regina Schubert, Jirka Jansch, Hans Scherhaufer, Ludwig Binder, Sebastian Schleicher, Hermann Kiessling, Thierry Bal, Marcus Bredt, Stefan Effinger, Peter Fürst, Claus Graubner, Brigitte Groihofer, Jörg Hempel, Udo Hesse, Rasmus Hjortshoj, Nina von Jaanson, Kasra Karimi, Emilie Koefoed, Vincent Mentzel, Elisabeth Niggemeyer, Jacques Paquier, Markus Pillhofer, Uwe Rau, Volker Renner, René Riller, Ali Schmid, Michaela Schöpke, Hans-Martin Sewcz

The Aedes Cooperation Partners are of substantial importance to the continuity of Aedes' work and success. For the long-lasting, friendly and synergetic partnership and thus also for the realisation of this publication we wish to thank:

Zumtobel   Carpet Concept   Schindler/The Port Technology   Cemex   Camerich   Baunetz

Dear friends, colleagues and readers,

It has been four decades since the Aedes Architecture Forum first opened its doors to the public as a one-of-a-kind experiment and grew to become one of the foremost private architecture galleries in the world. And what's more, this feat was accomplished by two women with no background in architecture. Was it crazy or naive? Frankly speaking, both. From the outset, Aedes was a collective effort and it still is; fuelled to this day by the passion of everyone involved.

With a shared conviction to communicate architecture and urbanism to a wider public through exhibitions and catalogues, Helga Retzer (†1984) and Kristin Feireiss founded Aedes in 1980. It has since become a globally recognised institution and exhibition space renowned far beyond the city limits of Berlin. More than 500 exhibitions and accompanying catalogues later, Aedes, co-directed by Hans-Jürgen Commerell since 1994, is still driven by the same impetus to promote a better understanding of the design of our built environment and its fundamental role in shaping the world we live in. By operating entirely without public funding since the beginning, Aedes has maintained a strong, independent position unimpeded by the political decision-making processes within the global and public architectural discourse ever since.

Always in search of new challenges, Aedes embarked on yet another adventure with the establishment of the Aedes Network Campus Berlin in 2009. Supported by its extensive personal partnership network – also within the academic realm – this metropolitan laboratory serves as a physical and intellectual platform focused on the inextricable interplay between urban form and social life. For more than a decade, it has brought international universities, civic and cultural institutions, policy makers, and industry and design experts together with the public to engage in a dialogue on architecture, urban design and culture.

Looking back on our forty-year development, the book at hand brings together some of the innumerable colleagues who have made it possible for us to persevere for nearly half a century: inspiring minds from across the globe discussing and arguing; exchanging knowledge and experience; sharing ideas, visions and dreams; and most importantly, building lasting friendships. As the title suggests, *Faces & Spaces* presents portraits and snapshots of our long-time collaborators alongside images of selected exhibitions from Aedes' entire programme archive. With never-before-seen photographs of architects, urban planners, artists, designers, sociologists, architectural historians, writers and curators actively engaged in discourse, this publication forms a unique visual record of recent international architecture history on nearly five hundred pages.

We would like to express our special thanks to all those who have accompanied and supported us on this exciting journey and undoubtedly helped to ensure our success. You are the reason we are able to celebrate our 40th anniversary and we look forward to many more years to come with you.

With deep gratitude
Kristin Feireiss and Hans-Jürgen Commerell

1980 1981 19
1985 1986 19
1990 1991 19
1995 1996 19
2000 2001 20
2005 2006 20
2010 2011 20
2015 2016 20

82 1983 1984
87 1988 1989
92 1993 1994
97 1998 1999
02 2003 2004
07 2008 2009
12 2013 2014
17 2018 2019

Aedes
Galerie für Architektur
und Raum

Helga Retzer
Kristin Feireiss

Peter Smithson
Dietmar Grötzebach

Stefan Wewerka
Alison Smithson

Peter Cook

Werner Düttmann
Josef Paul Kleihues

John Hejduk
Fritz Bornemann

Giorgio Grassi

Rem Koolhaas

Raimund Abraham

Lebbeus Woods

Peter Noever
Hans Hollein
Wolf D. Prix

Kristin Feireiss
Heinrich Klotz

Lukas Feireiss
Julius Posener

James Stirling

Cedric Price

Eduardo Paolozzi

Robert Venturi

Peter Eisenman
Kristin Feireiss

Álvaro Siza

Daniel Gogel

Kristin Feireiss
Aldo Rossi

Birgit Jürgens
Tanja Riccius
Karin Rühle
Marina Stankovic

Miroslav Šik

Frank O. Gehry
Lukas Feireiss

Vittorio Gregotti
Linde Burkhardt
Julius Posener

Josep Lluís Mateo

**Hans Kollhoff
Helga Timmermann**

Oswald M. Ungers

Frank O. Gehry

SPACES

Fehling + Gogel
Grundrißanalysen
Grolmanstraße

Fehling + Gogel
Grundrißanalysen
Grolmanstraße

Hans Dieter Schaal
Grolmanstraße
41

In Memoriam Kongreßhalle Berlin
Grolmanstraße

**Lebbeus Woods
Berlin Free Zone
Grolmanstraße**

Venturi, Rauch and Scott Brown
Laguna Gloria Art Museum
Grolmanstraße

1980 1981 19
1985 1986 19
1990 **1991** **19**
1995 **1996** **19**
2000 2001 20
2005 2006 20
2010 2011 20
2015 2016 20

82 1983 1984
87 1988 1989
92 1993 1994
97 1998 1999
02 2003 2004
07 2008 2009
12 2013 2014
17 2018 2019

Michael Mönninger
Christoph Mäckler

Wilhelm Holzbauer
Gustav Peichl

Shin Takamatsu
Gabriel Lahyani

Clorindo Testa

Richard Rogers

Will Alsop

Kristin Feireiss
Richard Meier

Bernhard Leitner

Thom Mayne
Kristin Feireiss

David Whitney
Philip Johnson

Kristin Feireiss
Peter Raue

Fritz Auer
Carlo Weber

Daniel Libeskind
Dietmar Steiner

Zaha Hadid
Patrik Schumacher
Kristin Feireiss

Michael Graves

Kristin Feireiss
Matthias Sauerbruch

Axel Schultes
Adolf Krischanitz

Norman Foster

Zvi Hecker
Hans Hollein

Stanley Tigerman

Peter Smithson

Günter Behnisch

Renzo Piano

Volker Schlöndorff
Frank O. Gehry

Bruno Zurkirchen

Daniele Marques

Günter Grass
Julius Posener

Manfred Ortner
Laurids Ortner

Roger Diener

Peter Zumthor

Julia Bolles-Wilson
Peter Wilson

Zvi Hecker
Massimiliano Fuksas
Otto Steidle

Lukas Feireiss
Hans-Jürgen Commerell

Dominique Perrault

Sergei Tchoban

Günter Zamp Kelp

Arata Isozaki

Benoît Cornette
Odile Decq
85

**Hilde Léon
Boris Podrecca**

Konrad Wohlhage

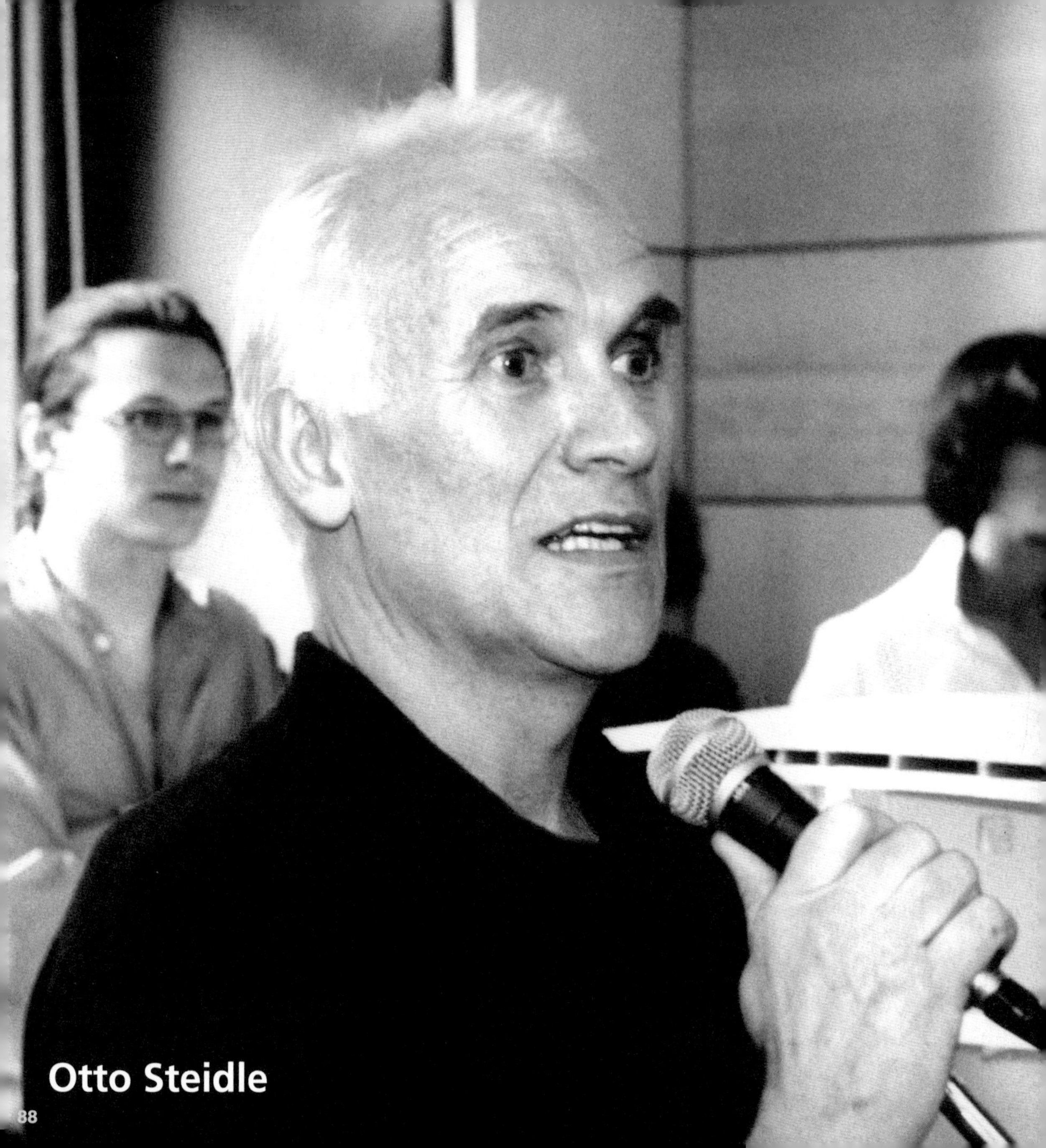

Otto Steidle

Kurt Forster

Andreas Brandt
Gabriele Schnitzenbaumer

Flemming Frost
Helle Juul
Abelardo Gonzalez

Ken Yeang
Yeohlee Teng

Elsa Prochazka

Hani Rashid

Armand Grüntuch
Almut Grüntuch-Ernst

Nicholas Grimshaw

André Poitiers

Hans Hollein

Christoph Langhof

Christoph Ingenhoven

Karla Kowalski

Kristin Feireiss
Itsuko Hasegawa

Winy Maas
103

Enric Miralles
Benedetta Tagliabue

Kristin Feireiss
Claude Vasconi

Kjetil Thorsen

Tadao Ando
Hans-Jürgen Commerell

Daniel Libeskind

Frank Barkow
Regine Leibinger

SPACES

Peter and Alison Smithson
Tischlein deck dich
Savignyplatz

Renzo Piano
Building Workshop
Savignyplatz
112

AMP Artengo – Menis – Pastrana
Morphological Architecture
Savignyplatz

Tadao Ando
Places of Contemplation
Hackesche Höfe

Nicholas Grimshaw & Partners
Ludwig-Erhardt-Haus
Hackesche Höfe

Szyszkowitz & Kowalski
Monster
Hackesche Höfe

Grüntuch Ernst Architekten
Einblicke Ausblicke
Hackesche Höfe

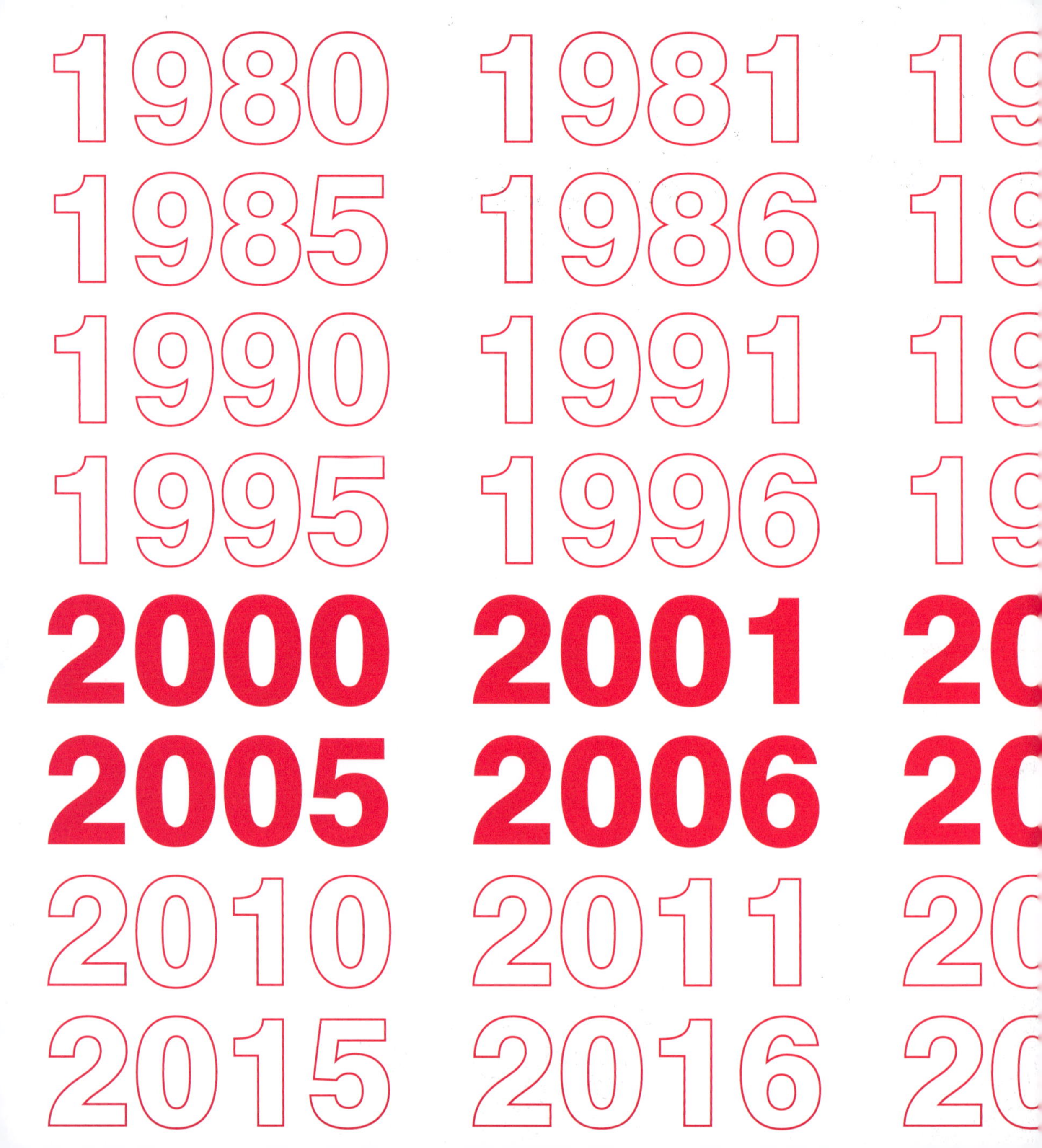

82 1983 1984

87 1988 1989

92 1993 1994

97 1998 1999

02 **2003** **2004**

07 **2008** **2009**

12 2013 2014

17 2018 2019

Hanns Zischler

Kristin Feireiss
Frei Otto

Johannes Kister

Wang Shu
Zhang Lei
Kristin Feireiss
Ding Wowo

Erick van Egeraat

Michael Mönninger
Yasmine Mahmoudieh

Arno Ledere
Marc Oei

Jórunn Ragnarsdóttir

Liu Jiakun

Kazuyo Sejima

Luyanda Mpahlwa
Peter Rich
Alun Samuels

Jo Coenen

Lars Spuybroek

Matthias Sauerbruch
Rem Koolhaas

Shigeru Ban
Kristin Feireiss

Hans Kollhoff

Ai Weiwei
Ma Qingyun

Peter Kulka
Gernot Nalbach

Zhang Lei

Tatiana Bilbao
Hans-Jürgen Commerell

Alexander Brodsky

Günter Behnisch
Hardt-Waltherr Hämer

Aaron Betsky

Ulla Giesler
Bimal Patel

Zaha Hadid
Kristin Feireiss
Odile Decq

Harald Szeemann

Bernard Khoury
Hans-Jürgen Commerell

Falk Jaeger
Stefan Behnisch

Lilli Hollein

Simon Ungers

Oriol Bohigas
David Mackay

Josep Martorell

Hans Ulrich Obrist

Yona Friedman

János Kárász
Maria Auböck

Kristin Feireiss
Harald Szeemann
Marion Taube

Roman Delugan

Elke Delugan-Meissl

Michael Riedel
Simona Malvezzi
Wilfried Kuehn

Werner Sobek
Dominique Perrault

Kamel Louafi

Ansgar Schulz
Benedikt Schulz

Inge Röcker

Jean Sundin
Enrique Peiniger

Hans-Jürgen Commerell
Kristin Feireiss
Gerhard Hannesen

Toyo Ito

Mohsen Mostafavi

Frank Barkow
Wiel Arets

Jörg Schlaich

Fernando Menis
Juan Lucas Young

Rebecca Chestnutt
Robert Niess
Hans Stimmann

Chang Yung Ho
Liu Sola

Ernst Ulrich Tillmanns
Alexander von Salmuth
Matthias Burkart

Wolfram Putz
Lars Krückeberg
Thomas Willemeit

Günther Vogt

Gabriele G. Kiefer

Jürgen Tietz
Johanne Nalbach
Kristin Feireiss

Rem Koolhaas
Madelon Vriesendorp

Thomas von Ballmoos

Ute Meta Bauer

Buzz Yudell
John Ruble

Reiner Nagel
Elisabete França

Hitoshi Abe
Kazuhiro Kojima
Manabu Chiba
Senhiko Nakata

Madelon Vriesendorp
Hans-Jürgen Commerell

Aravamuthan Srivathsan
Rohit Mujumdar

Neelkanth Chhaya

Anette Kolarski
Zvi Hecker

Angelika Fitz

Hubert Klumpner
Alfredo Brillembourg

Helle Juul
Wolf D. Prix

Regine Leibinger
Bruno Krucker

Hans Georg Esch
Christopher Dell

Naresh Narasimhan

Haewon Shin

Theresa Keilhacker
Hans-Jürgen Commerell

Luis Feduchi
Anupama Kundoo

Anand Patel

Erik-Jan Ouwerkerk

SPACES

Sauerbruch Hutton
What You See Is What You Get
Savignyplatz

Ai Weiwei
Traveling Landscape
Savignyplatz

The Rediscovery of Sretenka, Moscow
Savignyplatz

Re-Imagining Architecture
Savignyplatz

**Paju Book City
Dance Performance by Ahn Eun-me
Savignyplatz**

Paju Book City
Savignyplatz

Raumlabor Berlin
Eichbaumoper
Savignyplatz

207

Find the Gap
Hackesche Höfe

AustriArchitektur
Hackesche Höfe

Alexander Brodsky
Hackesche Höfe

Herzog & de Meuron
Instituto Óscar Domínguez
Hackesche Höfe

Swiss Shapes
Pfefferberg

Delugan Meissl
Intense Repose
Pfefferberg

Ólafur Elíasson
A Laboratory of Mediating Space
Pfefferberg

Graft
Graftworld
Pfefferberg

ADK München, Studio Maria Auböck
Der Dritte Raum
Pfefferberg

Wang Yiyang, Liu Sola, Yung Ho Chang, Liu Zhizhi
Creative Arts from China
Pfefferberg

Madelon Vriesendorp
Pfefferberg

Ursula Schulz-Dornburg
Tongkonan, Alang and the House Without Smoke
Pfefferberg

Zumtobel Group Award 2007
Pfefferberg

Von Ballmoos Krucker Architekten
Buildings and Speculations
Pfefferberg

1980 1981 19
1985 1986 19
1990 1991 19
1995 1996 19
2000 2001 20
2005 2006 20
2010 2011 20
2015 2016 20

82 1983 1984
87 1988 1989
92 1993 1994
97 1998 1999
02 2003 2004
07 2008 2009
12 2013 2014
17 2018 2019

Kazuyo Sejima
Kristin Feireiss
Martha Thorne

Vienna - Wiener Wohnba
ologisch
Dietmar Steiner

Kristin Feireiss
Gabi Schillig

Matthias Rick
Markus Bader

Francisco Mangado
Fuensanta Nieto
Diébédo Francis Kéré

César Pelli
Kristin Feireiss

Ton Matton

Manuela Luca-Dazio
Kristin Feireiss

Sustain
the Built Environ
Karin Zumtobel-Chammah

Michael Geschwentner
Patrick Gmür

Andreas Kipar

Peter Eisenman

Kazuyo Sejima

Markus Dochantschi

Momoyo Kaijima
Hans-Jürgen Commerell

Yoshiharu Tsukamoto

David Chipperfield

Floris Alkemade

Regula Lüscher
Karin Sander

Luis Berríos-Negrón

Iñaki Echeverria
Volker Halbach

Johannes Kuehn
Jan Edler

Robert A. M. Stern

Rem Koolhaas
Peter Sloterdijk

Ursula Schulz-Dornburg
Eike Roswag-Klinge

Colin Ripley
Thomas Auer

Anna Heringer

Tim Edler

Liz Diller

Diébédo Francis Kéré

Bernhard Marte
Herbert Resch

Mathias Klotz
Alejandro Aravena

Sarah Graham
Hans-Peter Achatzi
Marc Angélil

Peter Wilson

Tom Klingbeil

Hilde Léon
Regina Poly

Jean-Pierre Pranlas-Descours

Tom Kaden

Wolf D. Prix
Steven Holl

Dieter Kosslick

Henk Ovink
Winy Maas
Yoshiharu Tsukamoto

ANCB THE METROPOLITAN LABORATORY
Hani Rashid

Winka Dubbeldam
Almut Grüntuch-Ernst

Eric Owen Moss

Caroline Bos
Kristin Feireiss

Matthijs Bouw

Lijia Lu
Hans-Jürgen Commerell
Lu Wenju

Philip Ursprung

Arno Brandlhuber

Exhibition 30.05.-05.0
Ausstellung 30.05.-0
Sergey Kuznetsov

Rob Krier
Gottfried Böhm

Titus Bernhard

Roger Diener

Harald Müller

Enrique Sobejano

Fuensanta Nieto

Mathias Klotz

Martin Rein-Cano
Miriam Mlecek

Dani Karavan

Dietmar Eberle

Alexander Schwarz
Georg Vrachliotis

Mark Wigley

Mateo Kries
Rolf Fehlbaum

Hans-Jürgen Commerell
Juan Navarro Baldeweg

Álvaro Siza
Ursula Schulz-Dornburg

Shigeru Ban

Claudia Perren
Annett Zinsmeister

Beatriz Colomina
Nikolaus Hirsch

Kristin Feireiss
Thomas Willemeit

Julio Gaeta
Josep Ferrando
Luby Springall

Seung H-Sang

Julia Schulz-Dornburg
Ursula Schulz-Dornburg

Regula Lüscher
Álvaro Siza

François Burkhardt
Linde Burkhardt

Stefano Boeri

Lukas Feireiss
Andreas Gehrke

Francine Houben
Benedetta Tagliabue

Ben van Berkel

Frank-Walter Steinmeier
Ursula Seeba-Hannan

Kristin Feireiss
Bernard Tschumi
Beate Engelhorn

Josef Ostermayer
Bené Feireiss

Che Fei
Zhang Yue

Paul Friedli
Hans-Jürgen Commerell

Lukas Feireiss
Jürgen Mayer H.

Verena von Beckerath

Christoph Sattler
Volkwin Marg

Susanne Hofmann
Martin Wenger

Wong Mun Summ
Richard Hassell

Daniel Libeskind
Nina Libeskind

Louisa Hutton

Ilka Ruby
Dietmar Eberle

Zhang Ke
Anh-Linh Ngo

Volker Perthes

Eduard Kögel
Rocco Yim

Jürg Zumtobel
Josef Ostermayer
Nikolaus Marschik
Petra Wesseler

Heribert Wolfmayr
Josef Saller

Kristin Feireiss
Wolf D. Prix
Zvi Hecker

Odile Decq
Thom Mayne
Peter Cook

Kim Herforth Nielsen

Wang Shu
Kristin Feireiss
Lu Wenju

Sascha Suhrke
David Ausserhofer

Eckhard Gerber
Hinnerk Wehberg

Meinhard von Gerkan
Ian Ritchie

Stefan Marte
Bernhard Marte

Kristin Feireiss
Peter Cook

Isabel Zumtobel
Zhu Pei

Kristin Feireiss
Remy Sietchiping

Liu Jiakun

Richard Sennett

Saskia Sassen

Brendan MacFarlane
Dominique Jakob

Aric Chen

Enrique Norten

Thomas Trenkamp

Henry Pudewill
Georg Gewers

Yves Besançon
Pablo Larrain
Claudia Pertuze

Brendan MacFarlane
Philippe Etienne
Francis Rambert

Kristin Feireiss
Frank O. Gehry

Martha Thorne
Peter Cachola Schmal

ess:
Doreen Liu
Song Dong
343

Jan Krause
Christoph Felger

Ólafur Elíasson
Liz Diller

Niklas Maak
Reinier de Graaf

Farrokh Derakhshani
Wang Jun

Chris Dercon
Liz Diller

Philipp Misselwitz
Xu Tiantian

Annett Zinsmeister
Theo Deutinger

Ai Weiwei
Lukas Feireiss

Aaron Betsky
Thom Mayne

Matthias Hummel

Kjetil Thorsen
Zhang Ke
Herbert Resch

Deyan Sudjic
Sarah Miller

Sonja Mechling

Falk Jaeger
Bernhard Schulz

David Chipperfield

Fermín Vázquez
Ana Bassat

Christiane Sauer

Sarah Whiting

Andreas Ruby
Armand Grüntuch

Siegmar Hiller
Sonja Frank
Sophie Bleifuß

**Dulce Xerach
Fernando Menis**

Ou Ning

Lars Lerup

Christine Schraner Burgener
Dominique Perrault

Nicole Berganski
Andreas Krawczyk

Kamel Louafi
Hans-Jürgen Commerell

Hans-Jürgen Commerell
Ai Weiwei

Peter Jay Zweig

António Choupina
Álvaro Siza
Claudia Perren

Sergei Tchoban
Matthias Sauerbruch

Martin Roth

Jean-Paul Viguier
Angelika Nolte
Eike Becker

Li Xiangning

Sergei Tchoban

Martino Stierli
Ai Weiwei

Junya Ishigami

Dagmar Richter

Boris Schade-Bünsow
Heike Hanada
Jan Kleihues

Max Schwitalla
Tobias Nolte
William Menking

Bar Cafe
AEDES
Finn Geipel
Kristin Feireiss
Kaye Geipel

Wim Wenders
Kashef Chowdhury

Anna Popelka
Georg Poduschka

Alexandra Decker

Kim Young Jun
Hyungmin Pai

Jean-Louis Cohen

Kristin Feireiss
Gary Bates

Dorte Mandrup
Louis Becker

Ole von Uexküll

Christopher Dell

Róisín Heneghan

Christian Berg

Michael Verhoeven

Adrian von Buttlar
Johannes Robbrecht

Anna Ramos
Laura Martínez de Guereñu
Nikolaus Bernau

Miquel Adrià

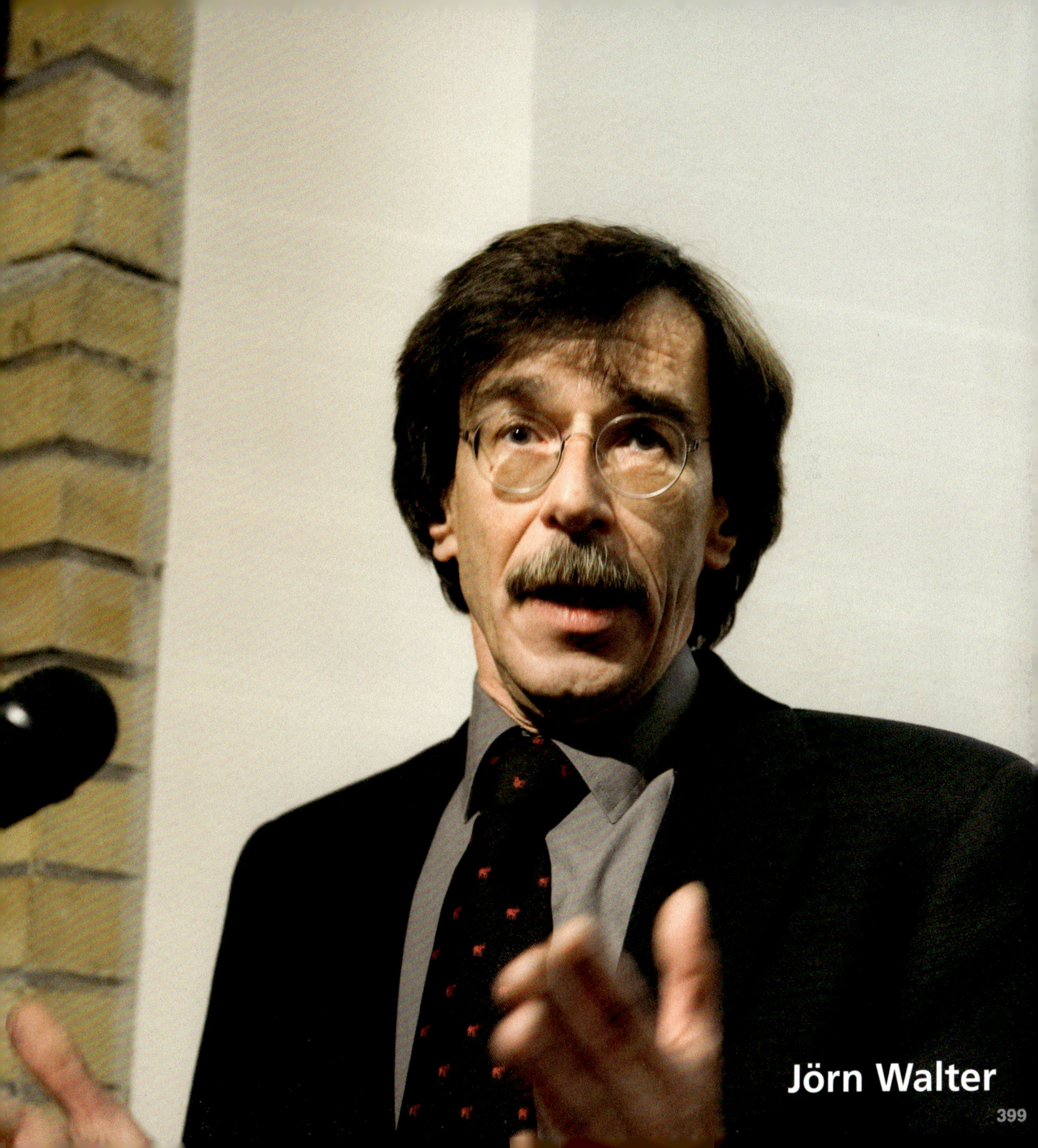

Jörn Walter

Maik Schlaich
Frank Breinlinger

Kristin Feireiss
Hartwig Fischer
Ursula Schulz-Dornburg

Piet Eckert
Wim Eckert

Bjarne Hammer

António Choupina

Anna Butele

Kristin Feireiss
Tatiana Bilbao

Johannes Robbrecht
Paul Robbrecht

Eduard Kögel
Friederike Meyer

Benedikt Jodocy
Davide Zampini

Christoph Hesse

Michael Schumacher
Jon Ritter

Wang Zaijian
Liu Xiaodu

Peter Böhm
Gottfried Böhm
Kristin Feireiss

Boris Brunner
Roger Weber
Elise Pischetsrieder

Moritz Dirks

Lale
Yüksel Pöğün-Zander
Jörg Zander

Francesca Ferguson
Ernst J. Wasmuth

Fu Haijun
Zhang Ke

Hans-Jürgen Commerell
Jacob van Rijs
Dan Stubbergaard

SPACES

Kazuyo Sejima + Ryue Nishizawa / SANAA
Pfefferberg

Vitra Campus
Architektur Design Industrie
Pfefferberg

Evol
Homework
Pfefferberg

ZAO/standardarchitecture:
Contemplating Basics
Pfefferberg

Collaboration
Across the Globe
— Quay Quarter
Tower, Sydney
CONNECTION
SPACE
3XN Architects
Behind the Scenes
Pfefferberg

Snøhetta
Living the Nordic Light
Pfefferberg

Volkwin Marg
The World of an Architect
Pfefferberg

Liu Jiakun
Now and Here – Chengdu
Pfefferberg

Diller Scofidio + Renfro
The Shed – Space on Demand
Pfefferberg

Ingenhoven Architects
Marina One Singapore
Pfefferberg
431

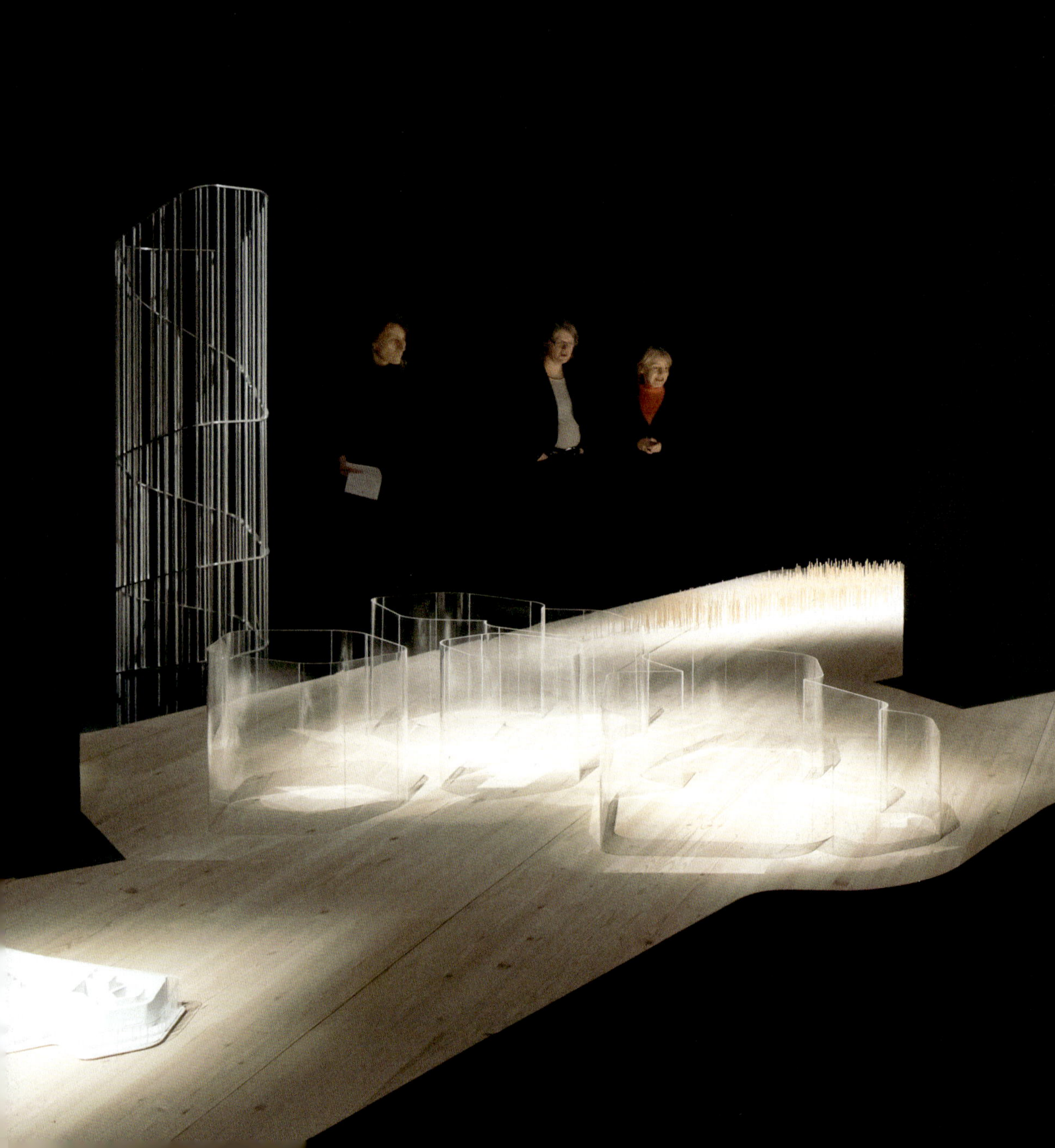

Nieto Sobejano Arquitectos
Tabula – Arvo Pärt Centre
Pfefferberg

Doreen Heng Liu, NODE Architecture & Urbanism
Shenzhen-ness – Space in Mutation
Pfefferberg

Christoph Hesse Architekten
Grounded
Pfefferberg

Dominique Perrault with SubLab, EPFL Lausanne &
ADSlab, EWHA Womans University, Seoul
The Groundscape Experience
Pfefferberg

b720 Fermín Vázquez Arquitectos
Enchanting Traces
Pfefferberg

Kashef Chowdhury/URBANA
Faraway so close
Pfefferberg

Ai Weiwei + Eid Hthaleen
Post Resettlement
Pfefferberg

Mathias Klotz
The Poetics of Boxes
Pfefferberg

DnA_Design and Architecture
Rural Moves – The Songyang Story
Pfefferberg
441

After Hurrican Sandy – Rebuild by Design
Pfefferberg

Iñaki Echeverria Arquitectos
Texcoco Lake Ecological Park, Mexico
Pfefferberg
443

Cobe
Our Urban Living Room
Pfefferberg

Form Follows Nature
Pfefferberg

Coop Himmelb(l)au
Pfefferberg

40 YEARS OF AEDES 1980–2020

A BRIEF TOPICAL OVERVIEW

Beginnings

In the late 1970s and early 1980s, Postmodernism was at its peak and the IBA Berlin (1978–1987) became the first International Building Exhibition dedicated not only to new constructions but also to conscious urban renewal and public participation. Against this backdrop, Aedes Architecture Forum opened in a forty-square-metre gallery space in 1980 on Grolmannstraße 51 in Berlin-Charlottenburg. Journalist Kristin Feireiss, who had been working at the International Design Center Berlin (IDZ), and Helga Retzer (†1984), who was active at the German Academic Exchange Service (DAAD), were neither architects nor regularly engaged with the subject of architecture in practical or theoretical terms when they founded Aedes. Their respective institutions only sporadically touched upon the topic of the built environment. In founding Aedes, both women were merely following their intuition that engaging in a discussion of architecture and urban space as important facets of everyday life with a broader public was a worthwhile endeavour: an open dialogue that would reflect changing societal conditions independent of questions of style and, most importantly, beyond expert discourses. Looking back on decades of successful programming since its inception, Aedes has itself become an integral part of contemporary international architectural history. While historically, major museums have presented exhibitions on architecture within broader cultural programmes, Aedes was the first public cultural space of its kind worldwide dedicated to the subject.

Independence

Under the co-direction of Kristin Feireiss and Hans-Jürgen Commerell since 1994, Aedes has developed a management structure as pioneering as its programme. With nowadays approximately 600 square metres of exhibition, event and office spaces combined, Aedes has remained an independent institution for contemporary architecture, urban design and related topics without public funding. By mapping a financially autonomous course, Kristin Feireiss and Hans-Jürgen Commerell have had the freedom to pursue their curatorial practice, the development of new formats and the expansion of their network outside of mainstream tendencies. Driven by the cutting-edge, best practices and visionary concepts from around the world, Aedes has presented the avant-garde, established luminaries and young talents in the field of architecture in over 500 exhibitions and counting, continually seeking, above all else, fresh ideas.

Venues

Reflecting its aim to reach a wider public, Aedes' exhibition spaces have been situated near the city centre and have always maintained free entry. The expansion of the Aedes 'universe' over time was dynamic. In addition to relocating to the S-Bahnbögen at Savignyplatz in 1988, the Hackesche Höfe in 1995 and Pfefferberg in 2006, Aedes' influence already transcended the borders of Berlin and Germany soon after its founding. Aedes also significantly shaped the development of the neighbourhood surrounding its present location in the former industrial complex at Pfefferberg in Berlin-Prenzlauer Berg, which has since become home to the studios of artists such as Ai Weiwei and Ólafur Elíasson, the Tchoban Foundation. Museum for Architectural Drawing and the ICI Berlin (Institute for Cultural Inquiry) – each with its own extensive networks of global impact. Adding to Aedes Architecture Forum's two exhibition spaces, the Aedes Network Campus Berlin, ANCB The Aedes Metropolitan Laboratory moved into the neighbouring building in 2009.

Outside of Berlin, Aedes opened temporary branches in Vienna from 1992 to 1993 and in Barcelona in 2004.

Exhibitions

With all its exhibitions, Aedes tries to develop new strategies and methods for presenting architecture to serve both a cultural and a societal dialogue. Exhibitions are no substitute for reality. They have to communicate complex subjects, and the public's cooperation is needed. Each show not only has to provide information, it has to stimulate a lively discourse on architectural design and urban development by being confronting, provoking and entertaining. A successful presentation requires a skilful combination of both information and enjoyment by using different kinds of media.

Catalogues

Along with most of the exhibitions, Aedes published a small square-format catalogue that has become an iconic trademark of the architecture forum since its opening days. Designed as a conceptual part of the programme by the renowned Berlin graphic design team Ott+Stein, for many young architects it was their first publication, and for the already established ones it has become a 'must have'. The first catalogue published was for the exhibition *In Memoriam Kongresshalle Berlin* in 1980, which was printed in a second edition, because of its success. That same year, the square booklets accompanied shows on the works of Peter Cook and Christine Hawley as well as on OMA's proposals for Rotterdam, followed by many others. In 1984, Zaha Hadid had her first international publication with an Aedes catalogue for *The Peak Hong Kong* exhibition. Over the past four decades, more than 450 titles have been published; some of them have reached the status of collector's items.

Funding

From Aedes' founding to the present, hardly any public cultural funding programmes have allocated financial support to architectural culture. As a result, Kristin Feireiss and Hans-Jürgen Commerell have fully embraced entrepreneurial and innovative funding paths, as well as the associated risks. Each project has to be realised individually through project-specific sponsorship or funding. For monographic exhibitions on architecture, sponsorship mostly comes from project partners, predominantly the construction industry. Financing for more thematically complex programmes is achieved through individual applications to foundations or other sponsors.

Cooperation

The worldwide reputation of Aedes as a cultural institution with a broad international network based on personal relationships affords companies seeking to expand their reach an attractive partner for the further development of products or services beyond their own circles. Businesses have become close cooperation partners through long-term commitments to support the work of Aedes as a leading international cultural entity, to jointly promote the amplification and dissemination of discourse on architectural culture and to create a broader awareness for the design of contemporary living environments. These international companies have coactively addressed questions surrounding the development of the built environment, mobility concepts, and living and working scenarios.

Dialogue

Aedes has been a critical conduit in fostering the international dialogue on manifold subjects regarding the urban environment, space and society. In creating an experiential cultural space in which the communication of architecture and urban/building culture could evolve into a genre of its own, Aedes developed new thinking spaces, curatorial concepts, techniques and formats for its mediation and discourse. The platform has become a reference point for innovative public educational formats for international museums, local architecture centres and cultural institutions from various fields. Aedes has established an international network of impressive depth and reach, which is shaped by the diversity of the presented ideas, strategies and designs. Together, these reflect an architectural, urban and cultural history of the late twentieth and early twenty-first centuries. The critical examination of established and speculative concepts of city, periphery, countryside and architecture is a core objective of Aedes Architecture Forum.

Berlin

The peak of Postmodernism shaped the 1980s, which the aforementioned International Building Exhibition IBA Berlin reflected. Aedes acted as a critical counterweight to the IBA, in part by providing architects, who had no or very little perception with a compelling space to present their positions. In this context, a young Zaha Hadid, virtually unknown at the time, showed her first exhibition at Aedes. Architects and offices such as Venturi Scott Brown, Cedric Price, John Hejduk, OMA, Peter and Alison Smithson, and Bernard Tschumi also presented their architectural and urban ideas and designs at Aedes. The first decade of Aedes culminated in two major exhibitions: *Berlin – Denkmal oder Denkmodell?*, part of *Berlin Kulturhauptstadt Europas 1988* commissioned by the Berlin Senate, and *Paris – Architecture et Utopie 1989*, commissioned by Jacques Chirac, then mayor of Paris. The exhibitions took place at the Kunsthalle Berlin and the Pavillon de l'Arsenal, with contributions by international avant-garde architects. As a topic of critical concern, the urban landscape of Berlin continues to inform exhibitions and discourses at Aedes, such as the development of the GSW high-rise on Kochstraße; the Alexanderplatz (1993) and Moabiter Werder (1995) competitions; alternative counter-designs for the Berlin Palace in Catherine Feff's mock-up palace (1993/94); the proposed Central Park Berlin by Christoph Ingenhoven (2001); and most recently, the petition to save the Mäusebunker and Hygiene-Institut buildings (2020).

Beyond

In striving to exhibit and discuss exciting examples of architecture and urban development from around the world in Berlin, the new and unique platform provided by Aedes in turn became an important international barometer for sophisticated design, planning and building culture. The 1988 exhibition *Berlin – Denkmal oder Denkmodell?*, curated by Kristin Feireiss, was subsequently shown in Paris, followed by Bern and the Eastern European cities of Krakow, Kiev and Moscow. Kristin Feireiss went on to develop exhibitions for the Kunsthalle Hamburg, the Deutsches Architekturmuseum (DAM) in Frankfurt, the Academy of Fine Arts Vienna and the Centre Pompidou in Paris. In recognition of her expertise, the growing reputation of Aedes and an expanding global network, the Ministry of Culture of the Netherlands named Kristin Feireiss Director of the Netherlands Architecture Institute (NAi) in Rotterdam in 1996, the largest museum for architecture worldwide at the time. During her tenure from 1996 until 2001, Feireiss brought important topics to the social discourse on architecture that significantly strengthened the museum's international standing. She introduced the NAi and its programme to a wider public and redefined the cultural and curatorial parameters of the organisation with exhibitions on architecture and spatial development in post-apartheid South Africa; the relations between city, periphery and countryside in Japan; and the significance of sports stadiums in the city, as well as through her contribution as commissioner of the Dutch Pavilion at the International Architecture Biennale in Venice, among many other important exhibitions. Large-scale and spatially experimental exhibitions spawned new formats of communication with a broad public impact and inspired architecture museums and institutions around the world.

Topics

While Kristin Feireiss was introducing local, national and global themes of urbanism and architecture to the agenda in the Netherlands, Hans-Jürgen Commerell was diversifying the programme of Aedes back in Berlin. Around the turn of the millennium, Aedes opened

Europe's view towards China. While Europe and the Western world went to China in pursuit of architectural missions, Hans-Jürgen Commerell asked questions about the state and identity of Chinese architecture itself, thus fostering the discourse on spatial production and the architectural identity of China's avant-garde since 2001. Another focus during that time was corporate architecture, which was presented in exhibitions on the DZ Bank by Frank Gehry, the competitions for BMW Welt and the Mercedes-Benz-Museum, and the architectural strategy of Louis Vuitton. Apart from monographic exhibitions, the focus also turned to the city as a social, cultural and political habitat: urban strategies of cities like Frankfurt, Johannesburg, Vienna, Seoul, Medellín, Paju, Mexico City, Moscow, Zurich, Thessaloniki, Almere, Singapore, Hong Kong and others were presented at Aedes.

Ecology

As discussions of green architecture led to concepts of sustainable architecture in the 1990s, Aedes absorbed this topic into its exhibition programme, drawing connections between societal demands for ecological processes in construction with new design questions and the renegotiation of the relationship between people and urban space. Aedes conceptualised and produced the touring exhibition *Made in Germany – Architektur und Ökologie* for the Goethe-Institut in 2004. Due to international demand, the exhibition travelled in two further iterations over the course of seven years to forty-eight cities around the world. In 2007, Aedes developed an international architecture award for the Austrian lighting manufacturer Zumtobel that connects aspects of sustainable construction with demands for better living standards and a healthier environment. Today, the *Zumtobel Group Award – Innovations for Sustainability and Humanity in the Built Environment* is an internationally renowned architecture award.

Digital

Beyond its pioneering role in highlighting sustainable architectural practices, Aedes has also been at the forefront of exploring the possibilities of the digital realm within the broader architectural discourse. In exhibitions and public talks that reach beyond questions of aesthetics, Aedes investigates the ways in which novel digital tools allow for an integrated and affordable approach in the design of new living and working typologies. Moreover, Aedes continues to explore the value sets in need of change in a global system of connectivity.

Arts

In numerous exhibitions throughout the course of Aedes' existence, renowned artists like Eduardo Paolozzi, Madelon Vriesendorp, Annett Zinsmeister, Alexander Brodsky, Dani Karavan, Ólafur Elíasson, Ursula Schulz-Dornburg and Ai Weiwei have presented a wide variety of artistic positions that deal with architectural and urban space in the contemporary cultural discourse in both critical and playful manners, and in a range of media, including installation, sculpture, photography, film, painting, illustration, music, dance and performance. The common thread of all these artistic explorations is the creation of new spaces of possibility and thought. At Aedes, the interplay of art, architecture and the city is both an object of discussion and an active mode of experience that consciously challenges conventional forms of architectural practice. In tandem with international contemporary artists, Aedes has explored architecture and urban planning as concrete manifestations of social, political, economic and cultural conditions, while examining how transformations of these conditions are manifest within society.

Education

An important step in the internationalisation of the
Aedes programme was the founding of the Aedes
Network Campus Berlin, now called ANCB The Aedes
Metropolitan Laboratory, initiated by Hans-Jürgen
Commerell in 2009. The starting point for this new joint
experiment was once again Aedes' strong network, built
over years of cultivating personal relationships, including
with many leading universities. At ANCB, global topics
are negotiated in a local context. This takes place, for
example, through exchange and experimentation in
multi-week workshops with architecture schools from all
over the world. Increasingly, international governmental
agencies, municipalities, foundations, embassies,
industry partners and institutions of civil society have
taken an interest in the transdisciplinary approach of
ANCB, resulting in new collaborations and formats.
Similar to Aedes Architecture Forum and its exhibition
programme, ANCB has shaped an international dialogue
that extends far beyond its physical borders.

Outlook

It so happens that the 40th anniversary of Aedes
coincides with a worldwide pandemic of unprecedented
proportions. In just a few months, the world has
fundamentally changed. Beyond the current crisis and
its as-yet-unforeseeable consequences, Aedes is aware
that the global challenges we are facing today and
in the decades to come are economic, technological
and political as much as they are social, cultural, legal
and ethical. These challenges demand a profound
and inclusive dialogue between all actors in society.
Aedes looks forward to continuing to actively provide a
platform for the much-needed conversations to come.

EXHIBITIONS

1980

Peter und Alison Smithson
Hauptstadt Berlin – Projekt 1957

In Memoriam Kongreßhalle Berlin
Realistische Phantasien und Realität

1981

Peter Cook, Christine Hawley, Ron Herron
Scenarios

Giorgio Grassi
Projekte und Entwürfe 1960–1980

OMA (R. Koolhaas, S. de Martino, K. Christiaanse)
Entwurf für ein Wohngebäude in Rotterdam

1982

Hans Dieter Schaal

Jasper Halfmann, Clod Zillich
Projekte 1976–1982

Gottfried Böhm
Marien Dom Neviges

1983

Werner Christian Wontroba
Zeichnungen, Installationen, Gruppenprojekte 62–82

Eduardo Paolozzi
Kunst und Bau – Architectural Projects

Raimund Abraham
Berlin-Projekte 1980–1983

Josef Paul Kleihues
Vier Projekte 1969–1980

Cork Mareschi
Kunst und Bau

1984

John Hejduk
Berlin Masques

Andreas Brandt, Yadegar Asisi, Rudolf Böttcher
Stadträume – Werkstattbericht 1982/1983

Zaha Hadid, London
The Peak

Coop Himmelblau
Offene Architektur – Ent-würfe 1980–1984

1985

Gustav Peichl
Zeichnungen & Zeichnungen

James Stirling
Wissenschaftszentrum Berlin

Álvaro Siza
Projekte für Berlin 1978–1984. Ein Skizzenbuch

Gezeichnete Utopien
Unrealisierte Projekte zur BUGA Berlin 1985

Coop Himmelblau
Skyline

1986

Cedric Price
Time + Timing. Projekte 1981–1984.

Peter Cook / Christine Hawley
Museum für moderne Glasmalerei in Langen
1985/1986

Grötzebach, Plessow, Ehlers
Projekte 1975–1985

Hans Poelzig
Ein großes Theater und ein kleines Haus

Meisterklasse Peter Cook
Städelschule – Architektur Frankfurt am Main

Zaha Hadid
Wettbewerb Adenauerplatz

Fehling + Gogel
Grundrißanalysen

Pietro Derossi
Projekte 1984–1986

1987

Christoph Mäckler
Bauten + Projekte 1985–1986

Meisterschule Gustav Peichl
Akademie der bildenden Künste Wien

Venturi, Rauch and Scott Brown
Laguna Gloria Art Museum Austin, Texas 1984–1985

Bernard Tschumi
Neues Nationaltheater Tokio

Architekturklasse James Stirling
Kunstakademie Düsseldorf

Lebbeus Woods
Centricity – The Unified Urban Field

Daniel Libeskind
One to the other – Arbeiten 1983–1987

1988

Andreas Reidemeister
Stadtkonzepte für Berlin

Meisterklasse John Hejduk
Cooper Union, New York

John Hejduk
Riga

Martorell, Bohigas, Mackay
Der Baublock 1958–1988

Synchrone Konzepte
Berliner Entwürfe für sechs Metropolen

Architekturklasse Hans Kollhoff
Eidgenössische Technische Hochschule Zürich

1989

Peter Eisenman
Guardiola House

Wettbewerb Amerika-Gedenkbibliothek Berlin

Meisterklasse Giorgio Grassi
Politecnico di Milano

Polnische Architekturzeichnungen der Gegenwart

1. Berliner Architekturpreis

Frank O. Gehry, Los Angeles
Vitra Design Museum

Architekturklasse Oswald M. Ungers
Kunstakademie Düsseldorf

Daniel Libeskind
Jüdisches Museum

Valeriy Bugrov
Kunsträume

Hans Kollhoff
Réalisations et Projets 1979–1989

Aldo Rossi
Deutsches Historisches Museum 1989

Nani Simonis
Bildräume

Peter Wilson, Raoul Bunschoten
Architectural Association – AA London

Junge Berliner Architektinnen und Architekten
Positionen

Julius Posener, Berlin
Mein Leben mit der Architektur

1990

Kas Oosterhuis
Artificial Intuition – Arbeiten am Computer

Technische Universität Berlin
Archen

RIEA / Research Institute for Experimental Architecture
The First Conference

Johanne + Gernot Nalbach
Die Ecke – 4 Projekte + 4 Bauten

Architekturseminar Gernot Nalbach
Universität Dortmund, Abteilung Bauwesen

Workshop Halensee Berlin
Berliner Forum junger Architekten II

Hans Hollein – Coop Himmelblau
Leitbild EXPO ′95 Wien

Hans Hollein
Ort und Platz

Morphosis
Rhythm/Movement – Project in Chiba, Japan

Zwischen Vision und Wirklichkeit
Neue Tendenzen in der Architektur der Sowjetunion

Wohnungsbau für die Hauptstadt Berlin
Fokus Berlin 1

Bernhard Leitner
Ton-Raum – Le Cylindre Sonore

TU Berlin
Ausgewählte Diplomarbeiten 1990

Wohn- und Geschäftshaus an der Paulsborner Straße
Fokus Berlin 2

1991

Peter Noever
The Pit

Lebbeus Woods
Free-Zone-Berlin. Entwurf für das Zentrum der Metropole

Szyszkowitz & Kowalski
Berlin – Graz. Two projects for research facilities

Richard Rogers Partnership
London, Tokyo, Berlin

James Stirling, Michael Wilford, Walter Nägeli
Werksanlagen der B. Braun Melsungen AG

Richard Meier & Partners
Canal + Headquarters Paris 1988–1991

Architekturklasse Christoph Mäckler
TH Braunschweig

El Lissitzky
Der Traum vom Wolkenbügel

Peter Stürzebecher. Architekturlabor Hamburg Partner
Ein Stadttor für Berlin, Wolkenbügel und Olympisches Ensemble

Foster Associates
Projects 1991

Shin Takamatsu
Drei Projekte

Bernard Tschumi, Ocular New York I II III
Columbia University

Peter Eisenman
Unfolding Frankfurt

Auer + Weber
Pavillon der BRD für die EXPO '92 in Sevilla

Wettbewerb Hauptpumpwerk Wilmersdorf

1992

Sauerbruch / Hutton Architekten
Projekte 1989–1991

Alsop & Strömer
Regionalparlament Bouche-du-Rhône + Neues Land für Cardiff

Daniel Libeskind
The Tenth Muse – Bürokomplex Wiesbaden 1992

Architektur – Wien zum Beispiel

Experimentelle Architektur

Entwurfswerkstatt TU und HdK Berlin
Workshop „Wohltemperierte Architektur"

Zaha Hadid
Vitra Fire Station

Hilde Léon – Konrad Wohlhage
Berliner Projekte 1992

Diener & Diener
Bürohaus Basler Versicherungs-Gruppe, Basel

Villenprojekt Meerbusch

Behnisch & Partner
Plenarbereich des Deutschen Bundestages in Bonn

Tigerman McCurry Architects
The Power House – Energy Education & Resource Center, Zion, Illinois

Schweger & Partner
Vier Projekte

Workshop Libeskind
Et Anelsens Observatorium – An Observatory of Premonition

Assmann Salomon und Scheidt
Berlin [bɛʁliːn]

Mit der Umwelt umgehen lernen
Beispiel Frankfurt: Wettbewerb Niedrigentropie-Kindertagesstätte

1993

Zvi Hecker
Heinz-Galinski-Schule Berlin

Beispiel St. Pölten
Eine Hauptstadt entsteht

Peter und Alison Smithson
Tischlein deck dich – Architekten entwerfen Möbel

Hollein, Zumthor, Ortner u.a.
Museumspositionen Österreich

Benedict Tonon
Morphologische Reihungen

Ben van Berkel
Crossing Points

Kleihues / Brenner / Lampugnani / Stepp
Kontorhaus Mitte. Friedrichstraße Block 109 Berlin

Das Schloss?
Entwürfe für die Mitte Berlins

Behnisch & Partner
Geschwister-Scholl-Schule Frankfurt am Main

Klaus Theo Brenner
Rummelsburger Bucht – Städtebau

The Growing Metropolis
Australian-German Experience

15 Years Architects at Aedes
Eröffnung Aedes East

Mechanical Landscapes
Bartlett School of Architecture London

HIC SAXA LOQVVNTVR
Gutachterverfahren Pfaffenberg

Positionen
8 Architekten

Yadagar Asisi
Berlin 2005 – Architektur-Panoramen

ARTEC Wien
Bürogebäude in Bludenz, Volksschule in Wien

Riegler-Riewe Graz
Nicht determinierte Architektur

Otto Steidle
Eine Universität und andere Wohnbauten

Edgar Lissel
Illusion der Macht. Berlin 1933–1945.

David Chipperfield
Houses, Offices & Museums

Dresden West: Intra et Extra Muros
Internationaler Architekten-Workshop Kaditz-Mickten

Steffen Lehman & Partner Architekten
Hülle – Schwere – Licht. Works and Projects 1990–1995

Becker Gewers Kühn & Kühn Architekten
Mix_t

Wettbewerb Torhäuser Leipziger Platz

Peter Zumthor
Stabwerk – Topographie des Terrors

Marques.Zurkirchen

Kunstpalast Düsseldorf im Ehrenhof
Planungsideen 1995

1996

Kister Scheithauer & Partner
Körper und Gehäuse

Peter Kulka mit Ulrich Königs; Ove Arup & Partners
Sportstadion Chemnitz 2002

Wettbewerb Erotisches Museum Berlin
In den Hackeschen Höfen

Zumtobel Staff & Sottsass Associati
Shadows

Neue Architektur für Bremen
Daniel Libeskind – Musicon; Gert Schulze & Partner –
Messe- und Veranstaltungszentrum am Bürgerpark

Ingenhoven Overdiek und Partner
Evolution Architektur Ökologie

Böhm Architekten
Gottfried, Dominikus, Elisabeth, Stephan,
Peter und Paul Böhm

Dominique Perrault

Baumschlager – Eberle

Tim Heide Verena Beckerath
Bilden

Don Bates
Workshop, After Geometry

Wien Architektur
Der Stand der Dinge – Zeitgenössische Bauten

Neue Architektur für Marzahn

Die Stadt im Comic
15 Zeichner sehen ihre Stadt

Lauber + Wöhr Architekten
Verwaltungsbau der Vereinten Versicherungen
München

Zamp Kelp
Mediale Aureolen – Projekte von 1987–1996

Warteschleifen
Ein Entwurfsprojekt von Architekturstudenten
der HdK Berlin

Zamp Kelp, Julius Krauss, Arno Brandlhuber
Neanderthal-Museum

Aus zwei mach drei
Neue Ansätze für ein Bauen in Zeiten knapper Mittel

Elsa Prochazka
Wiener Orte – 19 Arbeiten

Architekten RKW + Partner
Bauen im Bestand

Architekturzeichnungen
Sammlung Feireiss

Meisterklasse Wolf D. Prix
Prinz Eisenbeton – Auskunft aus der Zukunft

VISTA-Visualisierungsstudio für Stadtplanung
Bilder, Videofilme, Simulationen

Architekturfakultät Universität Venedig
Stadtvillen für Potsdam – Hommage an Ludwig Persius

Betz Architekten
Landeskriminalamt Berlin

Gabriele Schnitzenbaumer / Andreas Brandt
From the Temple Tomb to the Kennel

Monster
Kowalskis Tiere mit Gestellen von Szyszkowitz

Mensch und Architektur – db architekturbild
Europäischer Architekturfotografie-Preis 1995

1997

Erick van Egeraat
Cool Medium Hot

Werner Krömeke
Architekturbilder – Abbild und Interpretation

Sergei Tchoban
Der Java-Turm

Nicolaus Ott + Bernard Stein
Architekturplakat – Plakatarchitektur

Reiner Seliger
›z.ZT.‹

Thessaloniki, Kulturhauptstadt Europas
Zwischen Stadt und Meer – Acht Piers für Thessaloniki

ag 4 – Gesellschaft für Mediatektur
Projekt Hoechst Corporate Forum Frankfurt

Kees Christiaanse / ASTOC Architects & Planners
NL – D. Niederlande – Deutschland

Pit Kroke
Kunst im Stadtraum –
Skulpturen, Zeichnungen, Fotografien

Berger + Parkkinen
Nordische Botschaften, Berlin – Landschaft und Raum

Wissenschafts- und Wirtschaftsstandort Berlin-Adlershof
Wettbewerbsergebnisse in der Realisierung

Jourda & Perraudin
Contributions for Germany and other projects

Frank O. Gehry
DG-Bank, Pariser Platz 3, Berlin

Gerrit Engel
Buffalo Grain Elevators – Fotografien

Daniel Libeskind
Museum ohne Ausgang – Felix-Nussbaum-Haus

Itsuko Hasegawa
Fluctuations

Artengo – Menis – Pastrana
Morphologische Architektur

Jo Coenen & Co
Building the Territory 1987–1997

André Poitiers Architekt
Vier Projekte

Hiroshi Naito, Naito Architect & Associates
Silent Architecture

Embajada de Mexico en Berlin
Wettbewerbsergebnisse zum Neubau am
Klingelhöferdreieck

ST raum a.
in[zwischen]

Architekten Grüntuch/Ernst
Einblicke – Ausblicke

Jaume Bach/Gabriel Mora
From Reality into Reality

Auer + Weber + Partner
3 kulturelle Orte

db architekturbild 97
Europäischer Architekturfotografie-Preis 1997

1998

Bringing to World
Conceptionality and Intentionality in Architectural
Design

Gatermann + Schossig und Partner
Projekte

Thomas Weil
Geometrisches Ornament für Architektur und Kunst

Filmarchitektur – Production Design

Christoph Langhof
Atlas, Karyatide & Sphinx

Kamel Louafi
Die Gärten der Weltausstellung auf dem Kronsberg
EXPO 2000 Hannover

Elisabeth Lux / Frank Oehring
Pontormos Haus

Regina Poly
Plätze – Innenhöfe – Parkanlagen 1985–1998

Claude Vasconi
Architectures Europeennes

Hans Hollein + OMA / Rem Koolhaas
Zwei Botschaften für Berlin (Österreich/Niederlande)

Romuald Loegler
A Dialogue with Time and Place

T. R. Hamzah & Yeang + Yeohlee
Energetics: Clothes and Enclosures

Nicholas Grimshaw & Partners
L.-Erhard-Haus – Industrial Design

One Architecture
Urban Projects

transArchitectures
Cyberspace and Emergent Theories

Joachim Manz
Baustücke

Bangkok – City on the Move
Environment and Urban Development

8 & Willem
Junge französische Architektur

gmp / Meinhard von Gerkan
Architecture of Contemplation

Thessaloniki
Redesigning the Waterfront of Thessaloniki

Jourdan & Müller – PAS Freie Architekten
Frankfurt 2000 – High-Rise Development Plan

Josée Dionne
Yorckbrücken in Berlin

St. Pölten
Geburt einer Hauptstadt

de Architekten Cie
Ten Years 1988–1998

COOP Himmelb(l)au
Die Wiener Trilogie + ein Kino

Ernst Beneder
Zugänge – Eine monographische Werkschau

1999

Ortner & Ortner, Wien
3 Bauten für Europäische Kultur

EXPO 2000
Räumliche Visionen im Themenpark

Gottfried Böhm
Projekte

West 8
Engineer Meets Poet

MVRDV
100 WoZoCo's

Architektur in Bewegung
Entwürfe von jungen Architekten für Rotterdam

Léon Wohlhage Wernik – Urike Böhme
kunstbaukunst/ Oberstufenzentrum Berlin Köpenick

Jörg Pampe – Rolf Lieberknecht
kunstbaukunst/ Das Blaue Haus Berlin Tiergarten

Betz Architekten
Große und kleine Bauten – HypoVereinsbank, München

Stein Halvorsen
Karasjok – Berlin. Architektur 1990–1999

Gorski / Gothe / Van den Hoed / Schaller / Tchoban
Five Drawn Worlds

Ingenhoven Overdiek und Partner
Hauptbahnhof Stuttgart

Lina Bo Bardi
Eine Retrospektive

Guy Lafranchi
A.R.C.H.I.T.E.C.T.U.R.E.O.N.P.O.I.S.O.N.

Zug um Zug
Regierungsbauten in Berlin

Enric Ruiz-Geli
Spek*

Tadao Ando
Places for Contemplation

Snøhetta
5 projects

LOG ID
Grüne Solararchitektur

Barkow Leibinger Architekten
Cultivating the Landscape

Artware Edition – Architektur
Architekturgrafiken

db architekturbild 1999
Europäischer Architekturfotografie-Preis

2000

Chestnutt_Niess
The History of the Air

Klaus Kada
Raumkoordinaten

sauerbruch hutton Architekten
What You See Is What You Get

Artengo Menis Pastrana
Form and Matter + Las Maretas (Int. Competition)

Benthem Crouwel
Infastructure – Architecture

KSP Engel und Zimmermann Architekten
Presse- und Informationsamt der Bundesregierung

Tony Garnier – Albert Constantin
Une cité industrielle – Transformation

Henn Architekten Ingenieure
Corporate Architecture

Kamel Louafi
Die Gärten der Weltausstellung EXPO 2000 Hannover

Kovac/Malone, Australia
Political space

Nighthawk City
Architecture Students of the University of Westminster

OMA, Office for Metropolitan Architecture
Dutchtown Almere

Kister Scheithauer Gross, van den Valentyn und Schulz, Hillebrandt + Schulz
Bauten und Projekte in Halle an der Saale

Kazuyo Sejima, Ryue Nishizawa – SANAA
Recent Projects

Lederer + Ragnarsdóttir + Oei
Drinnen ist anders als Draussen

Zaha Hadid
Urban Architecture. Wolfsburg – Rom – Cincinnati

Daniel Libeskind / Barbara Weil
Mnemonic Cartwheels

2001

Ingenhoven Overdiek und Partner
Central Park Berlin

Das Berliner Schloss
Aufruf zu einem Moratorium

Kahlfeldt Architekten
Transformatoren – Transformationen

NOX Lars Spuybroek
NOX introduces the FLURB©

Diener & Diener
Die Schweizer Botschaft in Berlin im Spiegel anderer Projekte

Léon Wohlhage Wernik
Just Arrived – India and Bremen in Berlin

Alsop Architects
Not Architecture

LCM / Fernando Romero
Interpretations

Shigeru Ban
Recent Projects

Simon Ungers
Ferreous Forms

TU MU
Young Architecture of China

SIAT Architekten und Ingenieure
Bestimmte Bauten

Frederick Fisher and Partners Architects
Art Space

Najjar & Najjar
Kinematic Space

Peter Lorenz
CITY-NATURE – Buildings and Projects

2002

Cosy Concrete
Eine haustechnische Installation

Having a Wonderful Time: A City by the Sea
Prof. Andrew Holmes, Bartlett School of Architecture
and TU Berlin

Alexander Brodsky
Eine Installation

BMW Event- and Delivery Center
Architectural Competition

Topotek 1
Thinking + Working – Landesgartenschau Eberswalde
2002

Yasmine Mahmoudieh
Interior Design – Design as a comprehensive concept

double dutch
Absolventen des Berlage Instituts, Rotterdam

Wiel Arets
Blending

Jo Coenen
Housing the book – 7 Libraries

J. Mayer H.
Surphase Architecture

Mercedes-Benz Museum
International Architectural Competition Stuttgart 2002

Günter Behnisch
Ausstellung zum 80. Geburtstag

Behnisch, Behnisch & Partner
This side of Eden

Fremde in der Stadt
Klasse Prof. M. Sauerbruch, Staatliche Akademie der
bildenden Künste in Stuttgart

Peter Kulka
Poesie elementar

Werner Sobek Ingenieure
Beyond Materiality

Valery Koshlyakov
PackBandGlasPalast

Max Bächer
Gebaute Orte aus fünf Jahrzehnten

Joachim Manz
Wandstücke

Cruz y Ortiz
Architektur der Synthese

Claus en Kaan Architecten
beauftragt

2003

Baumschlager – Eberle
Of Regional and International 1996–2002

Pich-Aguilera Arquitects
Biopolis – Building Nature

Herzog & de Meuron
IODACC – Instituto Óscar Domínguez de Arte y Cultura
Contemporánea Tenerife

Peter Cook / Colin Fournier, Klaus Kada
Curves & Spikes – Kunsthalle und Stadthaus, Graz

Hans Hollein
Aufbauen und Aushöhlen

Michaela Habelitz
Lichtschnitt / Lightcut

Bernard Khoury
PLAN B – Projects in Beirut

BAU – Berliner Architektur Union
Arch Moskwa

INCLUSIVE
The Architecture of Louis Vuitton

Gernot Nalbach, Dimitra Figa
The First Sketch

Erick van Egeraat associates architects
For Russia with Love – EEA's Russia projects 2002–2003

Inea Gukema-Augstein
Blind Date

Ningbo
Metamorphosis of a Chinese City

Mirrored Metropolis
New Architecture and Urban Planning in India

G.L.A.S. ltd
Unser Berlin – Our Berlin

con_con 2003, China
constructed connections

Kees Christiaanse
The City as Loft

Karsten Sievers
quiproquo

Tadao Ando
Langen Foundation – Raketenstation Hombroich, Neuss

JUUL&FROST Architects
SIGNATUR – Dialogue Based Strategies of Design

Dominique Perrault Architecte
New Mariinsky Theater

Auke de Vries
After the Rain

2004

**Klaus Stattmann, the next ENTERprise,
Wolfgang Tschapeller**
Performative Materialism

Yona Friedman
Une vie spatiale

MADA s.p.a.m.
MADA on Site

Bernhard Strecker + Otto Steidle
Prora Polyphon

Itami Jun
A Korean Architect in Japan – Tradition and Modernity

Christoph Hildebrand
World Projector

Otto Steidle
Land Stadt Haus

Atelier Kempe Thill
Specific Neutrality

Drei Bauten von Karl Schwanzer
Fotografiert von Sigrid Neubert

MBM Arquitectes
Footprints in the City + Lost Architecture

Josep Lluís Mateo Architects
Organic versus Inorganic

Zerr Hapke Nieländer Architekten
turm – Dokumentationszentrum Berliner Mauer

Science City ETH Zürich
Hochschulcampus und Stadtquartier für Denkkultur

Architecture + Ecology
Made in Germany

Architecture + Religion
Made in Germany

Das Märkische Viertel
Idee – Wirklichkeit – Vision

Rüdiger Lainer
Ornament und die Tiefen der Oberfläche

Hans Kotter
Illuminations

Brunnert + Partner
Rethinking Airports

Wulf & Partner
all in motion

Oehringlux
' z '

Ursula Schulz-Dornburg
Architectures of Waiting – Photographs

3x Peichl & Partner
Neue Spitzen aus Wien

Christine Meierhofer
Das Aedes Aquarium

Titus Bernhard Architekten
Sensual Minimalism

2005

Ausgezeichnet
Handelsarchitektur aus NRW

Hans Poelzig
Bühnenentwürfe 1923–1927

5 German Landscape Architects
A touring exhibition for China

Auböck+Kárász
Gradual Landscapes – Open Spaces

Bewegtes Land
Internationale Bauausstellung 2000–2010
IBA-Werkschau 2005

Fast Forward Johannesburg
New Architecture and Urban Planning in South Africa

Sergei Tchoban / nps tchoban voss architekten
Berlin-Moskau – Neue Projekte 2003–2008

Quarks, Ziptown und Supersystem

Kühn Malvezzi
11 Projects

AustriArchitektur
Sieben Debüts aus Österreich

Rengin Holt
Transparencies

EMBT – Miralles Tagliabue Arquitectes Associats
Work in Progress

Studio Rocker
Re-Coded

Kamel Louafi
Der orientalische Garten in Berlin

Seung H-Sang
Culturescape

Paju Book City, Korea

KNOBS Design
Architecture Within

Schulz & Schulz
Wolkenlabor / Cloud Laboratory

Find the Gap
Neue Köpfe und Wege in der Architektur

Karl-Heinz Bogner
Objects

Rock over Barock
Young Austrian Architects

SLA
Wunderstadt. Participation – Planning – Urban Space

2006

Fernando Menis
Topography and Materiality

Neumann Gusenburger
OKZIDENT ORIENT Großer Tiergarten, Berlin und
Khalifa City, Abu Dhabi

WOHA and Mok Wei Wei + W Architects
More on Less / Chinese More or Less

Joachim Manz
Stadtstücke

Kister Scheithauer Gross
Typological Transformations – Conversion of a National
Emergency Reserve

Inge Roecker / ASIR Architekten+ ASIR Studio
Urbane Akupunktur

Volkwin Marg – gmp
Structure and Intention

Schlaich, Bergermann und Partner
Das Aufwindkraftwerk – Strom aus der Sonne

Ólafur Elíasson
A Laboratory of Mediating Space

**Palast der Republik – 'Cold War Museum' and 'Steel
and Freedom'**
Studentenarbeiten der Universitäten von Yale und
Columbia

Grüntuch Ernst Architekten
urban upgrade – Strategien städtischer Verdichtung

Zurich Happens & Swiss Shapes
Industrielandschaften im Wandel – Junge Schweizer
Architekten

Thomas Kesseler
Farbe und Raum

YO.V.A
Young Viennese Architects

TOPOTEK 1
Rauminstallation und Präsentation der Monographie
Paradise Remix

Delugan Meissl Associated Architects
inTENSE repose

Urban Think Tank Brillembourg & Klumpner,
Moderating Urban Density

www.plattformnachwuchsarchitekten.de
Stadt im Wandel – Stadt der Ideen

Behnisch Architekten + Transsolar ClimateEngineering
Ecology.Design.Synergy

Jong Soung Kimm
Tectonic Logic and Spatial Imagination

Johanne Nalbach
Soberly Sensually – 7 Townhouses for Berlin

2007

GRAFT Architekten
Graftworld – Szenografische Architektur

Haberland Architekten, Tilman Bock Norbert Sachs Architekten, Georg Scheel Wetzel Architekten
Orte der Adoleszenz

4a Architekten
Wasserwelten

Vogt Landschaftsarchitekten
Miniature and Panorama

Empresa Municipal de Vivienda y Suelo
Horizons – Madrid Social Housing 1981–2006

Büro Kiefer Landschaftsarchitektur
79 KW. – Opfikerpark bauen

AmP artengo + pastrana
The Mark of the Volcano

Manfred Sack
Tatsachen und Träume – Architekturportraits und Collagen

Ton Matton
The Climate Machine

Vorhang auf!
Sommerwettbewerb "Stadt im Wandel – Stadt der Ideen"

Deutscher Städtebaupreis 2006
Auszeichnung für zukunftsweisende Planungskultur und Stadtbaukunst

Wang Yiyang, Liu Sola, Yung Ho Chang, Liu Zhizhi
AND – Interdisciplinary Creative Arts from China

plan a
Überfunktion

The seventh room
Conceptual Urbanism in Zurich

Ai Weiwei
Travelling Landscape

Andreas Kipar
Zürichs Zimmer

2008

Baumschlager Eberle
Die Stadt im Haus

Titus Matiyane
Cities of the World, drawn panoramas

Madelon Vriesendorp
Flagrant Délit or Dream of Liberty

Zumtobel Group Award 2007
Präsentation der ausgezeichneten Projekte

Nieto Sobejano Arquitectos
arquitectura concreta

Erik-Jan Ouwerkerk
United City – Stadtbilder von Caracas bis Shanghai

A69 Architects
REMIXES

Pit Kroke
architektonische Skulpturen – skulpturale Architekturen

MVRDVH2O
water city projects

InSight USA
The New American Embassy in Berlin + Blueprint for American Prosperity. A Window of Opportunity + Shaping the Future

SPREE2011
Baden im Fluss. Mitten in Berlin

Latz + Partner
Bad Places and Oases

Dietrich | Untertrifaller Architekten
Rural Urbanism

Wilfried Dechau
Moscheen in Deutschland – Fotografien

nred architects
abstract natures

Ursula Schulz-Dornburg
Tongkonan, Alang, and the House without Smoke

Hans-Georg Esch
City and Structure

LINZ TEXAS
Eine Stadt mit Beziehungen

Siegrun Appelt
Einweihung der Lichtinstallation am Pfefferberg

2009

von Ballmoos Krucker Architekten
Bauten und Spekulationen

ohrenstrand mobil 08
Temporary architecture for new music

Charlie Koolhaas
True Cities – a photo(geo)graphic installation

Architektur: Portugal außerhalb Portugals

Andreas Kipar, Giovanni Sala + Partner
Raggi Verdi – Green Vision for Milan 2015

Der Dritte Raum / The Third Space
Installation by students of the Academy of Arts Munich

Seven Labyrinths from Madrid

Graber Pulver Architeken
Close-up

Werner Huthmacher
Portfolio – Sitzendorf, Leipzig, Beijing

Die Wiederentdeckung Sretenkas
Ein Moskauer Stadtquartier im Wandel

Europa Kai
The new dance theater palace quarter of St. Petersburg

MAGIC BLOCKS
Scenarios for socialist collective housing estates in Bucharest

What Makes India Urban?
Challenges towards Mobility, Infrastructure, Energy, and Perpetual Change

Kamel Louafi Landschaftsarchitekten
Urban Landscapes

Marte.Marte Architects
concrete works

2010

Seismograph City – Hamburg in Dialogue
sustainable strategies in architecture and urban design

Guiliani Hönger Architekten
Schnittwerk

Häfner / Jiménez, Büro für Landschaftsarchitektur
Land Lines

Office for Visual Interaction
Lighting Powers of 10

Zvi Hecker
Ein neuer Platz am Brandenburger Tor

raumlaborberlin (Jan Liesegang, Matthias Rick) u.a.
Eichbaumoper

Housing in Vienna – Wiener Wohnbau
innovative. social. ecological.

Eisenman Architects
Fragments of a City – Cidade da Cultura de Galicia

Veronika Kellndorfer
urban haze – reflect what you are

3XN architects
MIND YOUR BEHAVIOUR – How Architecture Shapes
Behaviour

Gabi Schilling, Architect and Artist
Public Receptors

Berlin Motion – Cinema of the Future
Workshop 'Cinematic Structures'

30/30
30 Projekte in 30 Tagen – HG Esch fotografiert Henn

The Informal City of Century XXI
A vision for the future of favelas in São Paulo

Measure of Man – Measure of Architecture
New Responsibility in Architecture and Urbanism

Zumtobel Group Award 2010
Präsentation der ausgezeichneten Projekte

Re-Imagining Architecture
Between Fact and Fiction

Membranes, Surfaces, Boundaries
Creating Interstices

Kazuyo Sejima + Ryue Nishizawa/SANAA
New Projects

2011

Cradle to Cradle® – Festival
The Next Industrial Revolution – Blueprint Netherlands

20 Under 45: The Next Generation, Singapore
A Selection of Works by Under-45 Singapore Architects

Gmür & Geschwendtner Architekten
Lost in Transformation – Geheimnisse des Wohnens

Kim Swoo Geun
Dense modernities – Korea's Architect for the Twentieth
Century

Arndt Geiger Herrmann Architecten, Zürich
Raum schafft Ort, Ort schafft Raum – Creating Space

Hans W. Mende
50 Jahre Mauerbau: Grenzbegehung

Cinema of the Future
Cinema and Urban Public Space

Water: Curse or Blessing!?
Encouraging Architectural Projects in Asia-Pacific

Singapore: City of Gardens and Water
presented by PUB, Singapore's National Water Agency

blauraum
wirklichwahr

Iñaki Echeverria
Cultural Ecologies: Texcoco Lake Ecological Park, Mexico

Francisco Mangado Architect
Architecture with the Left Hand

Form Follows Nature
A History of Nature as a Model for Developing Forms
in Civil Engineering, Architecture, and the Fine Arts

2012

schmidt hammer lassen architects
Give More

Kölner Ringstraßen
Drei Konzepte zur zukunftsorientierten Weiterentwicklung

Kaden Klingbeil Architekten
HolzWerkHolz

Pranlas-Descours
Architecture, Situations

Atelier Bow-Wow
In the State of Spatial Practice

FutureCityLab
Cities in Progress: Please Do Not Disturb

E2A Eckert Eckert Architekten, Zürich
Körper und Schichten

MACHEN!
The German Winners of the 2011/2012 Holcim Awards

agps
agps clues

New Frontiers
Zeichnen

White Mountain
Contemporary Chilean Architecture

COOP HIMMELB(L)AU / Wolf D. Prix & Partner
7+ – Projects Models Plans Sketches Statements

2013

Gottfried Böhm / Markus Böhm
Visionen

Diener & Diener Architekten + Gabriele Basilico
Common Pavilions

Julia Schulz-Dornburg
Modern Ruins, a Topography of Profit

UN Studio
Motion Matters

Smart City: The Next Generation
Focus Southeast Asia

Urban Think Tank
Beyond Torre David. Informal Vertical Communities

Architectonics
Bogota – Bottom Up Urbanism to design the City of the Future

Mathias Klotz
The Poetics of Boxes

Sanierungsgebiet Teutoburger Platz 1994 – 2013
18 Jahre Stadterneuerung in Berlin-Pankow

ArchiAid
Rethinking-Reconstruction The Great East Japan Earthquake

Titus Bernhard Architekten
(un)built ambivalence – House 11 x 11 and other projects

Gewers Pudewill
Structure and Experiment

2014

Andreas Gehrke & Markus Miessen
In-Between. Spatial Discourse in Visual Culture – Part 1 'Incertitudes'

Bau[t]en für die Künste
Zeitgenössische Architektur in Niederösterreich

be baumschlager eberle
Let's Build. From a Knowledge of Space / Vom Wissen über den Ort

Ursula Schulz-Dornburg
Photographs / Kurchatov – Architecture of a Nuclear Test Site

Álvaro Siza Vieira / Juan Domingo Santos
Visions of the Alhambra. New Access and Visitor Centre

Regina Poly
Mit der Schere gezeichnet

Vincent Fournier
In-Between. Spatial Discourse in Visual Culture – Part 2
'Infinities'

Gemeinde baut
Wiener Wohnbau 1920 bis 2020

New Moscow
Urban Development by International Competitions
2012–2014

Gaeta-Springall Architects
Building in the Metropolis MX

Josep Ferrando Architecture
matter & light

Vitra Campus – An Anniversary
Architecture Design Industry

Seoul: Towards a Meta-City
Recent Urban Projects in Seoul

Rubén Dario Kleimeer, Raul Walch, Marie Rømer Westh
In-Between. Spatial Discourse in Visual Culture – Part 3
'Ideals'

Mecanoo architecten
A People's Palace – The Library of Birmingham

Barcelona Re.Set
The Work of the Enric Miralles Foundation

Inflexión / Turning Point
The Transformation Process in Spanish Architecture

After Hurricane Sandy – Rebuild by Design
Resilient Planning through Collaborative Design

2015

Evol
In-Between, Spatial Discourse in Visual Culture – Part 4
'Homework'

ZAO/standardarchitecture
Contemplating Basics

Alps Architecture Tourism
New Architecture of the Landscape in South Tyrol

gmp Architekten von Gerkan, Marg und Partner
On Old Foundations. Building in a Historical Context

Medellín: Topography of Knowledge
Urban Tranformation Through Collective Processes

Lighting Planners Associates
Nightscape 2050 – A Dialogue Between Cities. Light.
People

Snøhetta
Living the Nordic Light

Rocco Design Architects
Intensity

heri&salli architekten
Architektur im Schlaf

Marte.Marte Architects
Appearing Sculptural

2016

Henke Schreieck Architekten, RLP Rüdiger Lainer + Partner, Walter Stelzhammer, Albert Wimmer
Ein Raum für Fünf. 20 Architekturjahre

RDAI Architecture Studio Paris
Zoom: From Object to Architecture

Change of Perspectives
Seven positions in contemporary architectural
photography

3XN Architects
Behind the Scenes – The Simplicity and Complexity of
Architecture

Kontinuum und Schnitt
Die Düsseldorfer U-Bahn 'Wehrhahn-Linie' –
ein Gesamtkunstwerk

Das Wiener Modell
Wohnbau für die Stadt des 21. Jahrhunderts

Buildings for Science and Culture
Revitalization of the Gdynia Seaport / Poland

Zài Xing Tu Mù
Sixteen Chinese Museums – Fifteen Chinese Architects

Ai Weiwei + Eid Hthaleen
Post Resettlement

Volkwin Marg
Die Welt eines Architekten. Zum 80. Geburtstag

LenzWerk
Die Entdeckung und Sanierung von Haus Buchthal,
Berlin

Zwischen Kunst und Politik
Wandteppiche aus der DDR von 1955 bis 1989

50 Jahre Gerber Architekten
Meilensteine aus fünf Jahrzehnten

2017

Unlakecity – Where There Was a Lake, Now There is a City
Geography and Architecture of Mexico City

Studio Zhu-Pei, Beijing
Mind Landscapes

Jakob + MacFarlane
Augmenting the Invisible

New Housing for Berlin!
Projects by HOWOGE Wohnungsbaugesellschaft

Constructing Culture
West Kowloon Cultural District, Hong Kong

Houston: Genetic City
Envisioning a Future Post-Industry, Post-Oil, Post-Sprawl

Liu Jiakun
Now and Here – Chengdu

Platform for Architecture + Research / PAR
Relations

Diller Scofidio + Renfro
The Shed – Space on Demand

ingenhoven architecs
'Green Heart' – Marina One Singapore – Architecture for
Tropical Cities

Nieto Sobejano Arquitectos
TABULA – Arvo Pärt Centre

PPAG architects
Do You Really Want to Live Like Your Mother?

**Dominique Perrault with SubLab, EPFL
Lausanne & ADSlab, EWHA Womans University**
The Groundscape Experience

2018

**Harvard Mellon Urban Initiative and
Graduate School of Design, Harvard University**
Urban Intermedia: City, Archive, Narrative

Xu Tiantian, DnA_Design and Architecture
Rural Moves – The Songyang Story

NKBAK Architects
Pushing the Limits

NODE Architecture & Urbanism
SHENZHEN-ness: Space in Mutation. Curated by Doreen
Heng Liu

falkeis²architects
Active Building – Innovation for Architecture in Motion

Woodland Sweden
Contemporary Timber Construction

Heilbronn – Eine Stadt erfindet sich neu
Bundesgartenschau 2019, Bildungscampus und experimenta

Fernando Menis
Backstage

b720 Arquitectos
Enchanting Traces

2019

Kashef Chowdhury / URBANA, Bangladesh
Faraway so Close

Archi-Tectonics / Winka Dubbeldam & Justin Korhammer
Flat Lands & Massive Things – From NL to NYC & Beyond

Tatiana Bilbao / A Collective Academic Initiative
Two Sides of the Border: Reimagining the Mexico-United States Region

Building a Future Countryside in China
Curated by Li Xiangning, Shanghai

Jean-Paul Viguier et Associés
INTENCITY

Gerber Architekten
Konzept + Atmosphäre

ZUKUNFT Schulbau
European examples of contemporary school architecture

Dorte Mandrup
HUMAN:NATURE – presented by AW Architektur & Wohnen

Anna Butele, Annvil
100 Experiments / Inspiration in Design Processes

Álvaro Siza
Pavilion for Camerich at the China International Furniture Fair (CIFF 2019) in Shanghai

Christoph Hesse Architekten
Grounded

Ritter Schumacher Architekten
Rural Uplift

weberbrunner architekten zürich & berlin
Holzgeschichten

2020

Stall.Schlachthaus.Fleischerei
Architektur für Schweine

Russian Biennale for Young Architects
Redevelopment of Industrial Sites in Tatarstan

Cobe
Our Urban Living Room

OBEL AWARD 2019
Water Garden by Junya Ishigami

APPENDIX

The Aedes Team

Christine Meierhofer
Personal Assistant to
the Director

Ramona Kleinfeldt
Executive Secretary,
Accounting

Dunya Bouchi
Managing Director
ANCB

Miriam Mlecek
Programme Manager
ANCB

Mathias Schnell
Project Manager,
Curator

Esenija Bannan
Project Manager,
Curator

All team members since 1980

Erika Alexander	**Ulla Giesler**	**Christian Oppert**
Thomas Alperstädt	**Ingeborg Gloxin**	**Nora Ouwerkerk**
Elisabeth Asefa	**Benedikt Gnadt**	**Andrew Pasaol**
Esenija Bannan	**Oliver G. Hamm**	**Kai Pfeiffer**
Ricarda Bethke	**Jutta Hörig**	**Andres Ramirez**
Julia Bischoff	**Ondrej Hojda**	**Christiane Raack**
Jürgen Bode	**Ilse Kischlat**	**Miriam Reichwaldt**
Silke Bosetti	**Ramona Kleinfeldt**	**Michael Roper**
Dunya Bouchi	**Barbara Koch**	**Áine Ryan**
Helga Brandenburg	**Eduard Kögel**	**Vincent Sauer**
Marcus Bull	**Friederike Krentz**	**Angelika Schlender**
Helmut Buttkus	**Christine Kuhnert-Güzel**	**Lothar Schnebel**
Chris Cockrell	**Joyce Labuch**	**Mathias Schnell**
Jakob Dannenfeldt	**Klaus Lakomski**	**Clea Stanischewsky**
Christina Delius	**Victor Laub**	**Tina Steiger**
Joanna Doherty	**Ricardo Lashley**	**Katharina Ström**
Kathrin Dröppelmann	**Jan Livschitz**	**Christian Thomas**
Julian Dueck	**Wolfgang Lösel**	**Alexandra von Stosch**
Pelle Dwertmann	**Roberta Lucchi**	**Hannes von Wuntsch**
Christine Eiselen	**Christine Meierhofer**	**Patrick Voss**
Gesine Elliger	**Mirko Mielke**	**Gabriele Weber-Domaschke**
Beate Engelhorn	**Miriam Mlecek**	**Boris von Wedel**
Klaus Engnath	**Isolde Nagel**	**Christel Weiß**
Marius Farwig	**Lena Nalbach**	**Eva Wildhardt**
Kate Fasano	**Moritz Nalbach**	**Vera Yu**
Sven Funcke	**Mattis Obermann**	**Dina Zoesmar**

Partners

For their generous and continuous support and collaboration, we thank the Aedes Cooperation Partners.
Read more about this synergetic partnership on page 450.

Photo Credits

Nina von Jaanson: pages 8, 9
Ludwig Binder: pages 10, 11, 13
Regina Schubert: pages 12, 19, 22, 26, 30, 31, 32, 34, 35, 50, 52, 53, 55, 56, 60, 61, 62, 65, 66, 67, 69, 70, 71, 72, 73, 75, 76, 77, 78, 79, 80, 82, 83, 84, 86, 87, 89, 91, 94, 98, 99, 105
Erik–Jan Ouwerkerk: pages 15, 106, 108, 109, 124, 128, 129, 130, 133, 135, 139, 142, 143, 148, 151, 152, 153, 154, 155, 156, 158, 159, 161, 162, 163, 165, 170, 171, 172, 173, 175, 176, 177, 178, 179, 180, 183, 184, 185, 186, 188, 189, 190, 192, 193, 195, 198, 225, 226, 228, 233, 235, 237, 238, 239, 240, 241, 242, 243, 244, 245, 247, 248, 249, 250, 251, 252, 253, 254, 255, 256, 257, 258, 259, 260, 261, 262, 263, 266, 267, 270, 271, 273, 274, 275, 276, 277, 278, 280, 281, 283, 284, 285, 289, 290, 291, 292, 295, 296, 298, 301, 304, 305, 306, 307, 308, 309, 311, 312, 313, 314, 315, 316, 317, 318, 319, 320, 321, 322, 325, 325, 327, 328, 334, 335, 336, 337, 339, 340, 342, 345, 346, 348, 349, 355, 357, 358, 359, 360, 361, 362, 363, 364, 365, 366, 367, 368, 369, 372, 373, 375, 376, 377, 381, 383, 384, 385, 387, 389, 393, 396, 397, 398, 399, 400, 401, 403, 404, 405, 408, 409, 410, 411, 412, 414, 415, 416, 417, 430, 431, 432, 433, 434, 435, 436, 437, 438, 441
Brigitte Groihofer, Architekturzentrum Wien, Sammlung: page 17
Riba Collections: page 23
Hans–Jürgen Commerell: pages 27, 44, 48, 49, 51, 74, 81, 84, 85, 90, 92, 96, 103, 109, 111, 112, 113, 114, 115, 116, 117, 130, 138, 140, 147, 157, 201, 214, 231, 264, 288, 299, 303, 324, 332, 347, 354, 355, 356, 388, 391, 406, 407
Elisabeth Niggemeyer: page 28
Peter Fürst: page 36
Uwe Rau: page 37
Hermann Kiessling: pages 39, 40, 41

Udo Hesse: page 45
Hans–Martin Sewcz: page 54
Sebastian Schleicher: pages 57, 63, 68
Elsa Prochazka: page 93
André Poitiers: page 97
Benedetta Tagliabue: page 104
KC²: 118
Jörg Hempel: page 119
Bauwelt: page 123
Vincent Mentzel: page 126
Jirka Jansch: pages 187, 224, 236, 269, 279, 286, 287, 293, 294, 297, 300, 302, 338, 350, 351, 352, 371, 382, 421, 422, 440, 442
Claus Graubner: page 210
Stefan Effinger: page 232
Michaela Schöpke: page 265
Isabel Zumtobel: page 329
Hans Scherhaufer: pages 331, 398, 427, 429
Jacques Paquier: page 333
V&A, Thierry Bal: page 374
Emilie Koefoed: page 379
Volker Renner: page 390
Ali Schmid: pages 394, 395
Kristin Feireiss: page 413
René Riller: pages 424, 425
Kasra Karimi: page 426
Marcus Bredt: page 428
Rasmus Hjortshoj: page 444
Markus Pillhofer: pages 446, 447
Aedes: all other pages

Imprint

Concept
Kristin Feireiss and Hans-Jürgen Commerell,
Aedes Architecture Forum, Berlin

Design
Christine Meierhofer, Aedes Architecture Forum, Berlin

Lithography, printing and binding
Europrint, Berlin

© 2020 Aedes and Park Books AG, Zurich

© for the photos: see page 479

Publisher
Park Books
Niederdorfstrasse 54, 8001 Zurich, Switzerland
www.park-books.com

Park Books is being supported by the Federal Office of
Culture with a general subsidy for the years 2016–2020.

All rights reserved; no part of this publication may be
reproduced, stored in a retrieval system or transmitted
in any form or by any means, electronic, mechanical,
photocopying, recording, or otherwise, without the prior
written consent of the publisher.

ISBN 978-3-03860-216-3